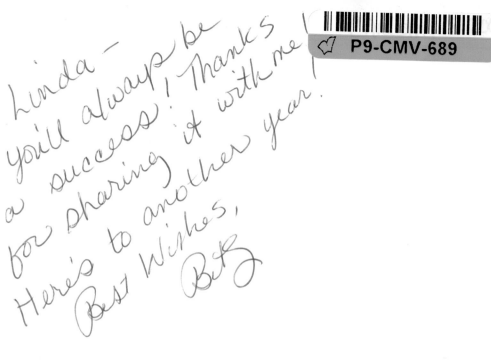

Linda —
you'll always be
a success! Thanks
for sharing it with me!
Here's to another year!
Best Wishes,
Bob

EXPECT SUCCESS

Compiled by Dan Zadra
Designed by Steve Potter and Jenica Wilkie

COM·PEN´·DI·UM™
Publishing

*E*nriching the lives of millions, one person at a time.™

ACKNOWLEDGEMENTS

These quotations were gathered lovingly but unscientifically over several years and/or contributed by many friends or acquaintances. Some arrived—and survived in our files—on scraps of paper and may therefore be imperfectly worded or attributed. To the authors, contributors and original sources, our thanks, and where appropriate, our apologies. —The editors

WITH SPECIAL THANKS TO

Jason Aldrich, Gerry Baird, Jay Baird, Justi Baumgardt, Neil Beaton, Doug Cruickshank, Jim Darragh, Kari Cassidy-Diercks, Kyle Diercks, Josie and Rob Estes, Jennifer Hurwitz, Dick Kamm, Liam Lavery, Connie McMartin, Janet Potter & Family, Diane Roger, Cristal Spurr, Sam Sundquist, Heidi Wills, Kobi Yamada, Robert & Val Yamada, Tote Yamada, Anne Zadra, and August & Arline Zadra

CREDITS

Compiled by Dan Zadra
Designed by Steve Potter and Jenica Wilkie

*Care enough for a result,
and you will almost
certainly attain it.*

—William James

EXPECT SUCCESS

*I believe you can have
everything you want out of life
if you just help enough other people
get what they want out of life.*

—Zig Ziglar

This is a book about mutual success. It's about creating real value and developing phenomenal relationships with our customers. The premise is that the fastest way for a company to succeed is to first ensure that everything you think, do, say or deliver is intentionally designed to help your customers succeed.

Wherever you look these days you'll find that the leading companies are not focused on increasing the number of their short-term transactions; they are far more interested in enhancing the quality of their long-term customer relationships.

Look up the word "relationship" in the dictionary and you'll discover that it means "an ongoing affair between two parties." Customer relationships are ongoing affairs. Good customer relationships are long-term affairs. The best customer relationships are, in a very real sense, long-term "love affairs."

It's true. In business terms, love is nothing more than continuously demonstrating sincere and massive "liking" for your customer. It's pretty simple really. All other things being equal, your customers will naturally go where they feel massively liked, loved and cared for.

The greatest love affairs are built on trust, sincerity and constancy. Constancy comes from the Latin, "com" (which means "together") and "stare" (which means "to stand"). There you have it. The golden key to those cherished long-term customer relationships is, quite simply, to "stand together" with your customer through thick and thin. And not just once in awhile, but every single solitary time.

Dan Zadra

HE FIRE

**Make your passion
your profession.**

—Carl Holmes

*We all need to believe in
what we are doing.*

—Allan D. Gilmour

*To love what you are doing.
To believe in what you are doing.
To know what you are doing.
These are the three essentials.*

—Steve Musseau

*When you know what you
are doing, and you care
deeply about it—and what
you are doing is the best—
that is inspiration.*

—Robert Bresson

EXPECT

*High expectations are
the key to everything.*
—Sam Walton

*It is our attitude at the beginning
of a difficult task which, more
than anything else, will affect
its successful outcome.*
—William James

*If you want to do something, you
find a way. If you don't want to
do something, you find an excuse.*
—Jeff Goforth

Success is an inside job.

—Ralph Ford

Passion begins on the inside of a person or an organization and then works its way out.

—Bob Moawad

Strong corporate cultures come from within, and they are built by every person inside the company, not by consultants.

—Craig R. Hickman

EXPECT

Great companies, great cities, and Nobel-winning efforts are all unfailingly led by people with a consuming passion for their discipline, product or customer.
—Tom Peters

The essential difference in service is not machines or things—it is minds, hearts, spirits and souls.
—Herb Kelleher, Southwest Air

The business of business is to keep the company alive and breathlessly excited, to be a force for good for its customers, and contribute something of value to the community.
—Anita Roddick, The Body Shop

The best companies assume that each individual wants to make a difference in the world and be respected. Is that a surprise?

—Paul Ames

People say, "Don't take business personally,"—but that's my work, my sweat, my time away from my family— how can that not be personal?

—Elaine Branson

If people relate to the company they work for, if they form an emotional tie to it and buy into its dreams, they will pour their heart into making it better.

—Howard Schultz, Starbucks

EXPECT

The height of your accomplishment will equal the depth of your convictions.
—William F. Scolavino

The success or failure of any company boils down to one question: Are you operating from passion? If you are, you're going to succeed. If you believe in what you're doing, you're going to make sure that everyone around you believes in it too.
—Maggie Hughes

Commit to your job and your work, whatever it is. If you love your work, you'll be out there every day trying to do the best you can, and pretty soon everybody around will catch the passion from you.
—Sam Walton

It's time to start thinking with the heart.

—Beverley Wilson

There is one thing we can do, and the best people and the best companies do this. We can be completely present. We can be all here. We can give all our attention to the opportunity before us.

—Mark Van Doren

Fascination is a key to productivity; it unites experiences; it is even its own reward.

—Erving Polster

EXPECT

Caring is the ultimate competitive advantage.
—Ron Kendrick

When the crunch comes, people cling to those they know they can trust—those who are not detached, but involved.
—Admiral James Stockdale

Enthusiasm reflects confidence, spreads good spirit, raises morale, arouses loyalty, and laughs at adversity...it is beyond price.
—Allan Cox

SET THE S

TANDARD

The principle was right there—you couldn't miss it. The more we did for our customers, the more they did for us.

—Debbi Fields

Every great business is built on friendship.

—J.C. Penney

We are closest to our customers when we help them grow and succeed.

—Michael Nolan

Successful people are always looking for opportunities to help others. Unsuccessful people are always asking, "What's in it for me?"

—Brian Tracy

EXPECT

A sale is not something you pursue; it's what happens to you while you are immersed in the act of serving your customer.

—Jim Williamson

All of us are the company, and each of us must be committed to providing superior value and personalized service every single time to our customers.

—Jay Medica

"Satisfied" customers isn't good enough anymore—we have to create raving fans!

—Jon May

The real issue is value, not price.

—Robert T. Lindgren

There are so many people who can figure costs, and so few who can measure value.

—Dick Kamm

Which is more important—great quality, or great service? The answer is neither. The objective is great customer value—the total combination of things and experiences that create a total customer perception of value received—each time, every time.

—Karl Albrecht

EXPECT

*When real value is created,
the whole world profits.*
—Scott Johnson

*Financial Success is producing
sufficient revenue above your
expenses to meet or exceed your
revenue goals while having customers
who are thrilled with the value of your
products and service.*
—Mark Leskovar

*Better quality + lesser price =
value + spiritual attitude of our
employees = unbeatable.*
—Herb Kelleher, Southwest Airlines

The quality of any product or service is what the customer says it is.

—Techsonic

First and foremost and in everything we do daily, ask: "If I were the customer—would I buy it? If I were the customer, would the service I provided fulfill my expectations?"

—Mark Pinnetti

The two most important words I ever wrote were on that first Wal-Mart sign: "Satisfaction Guaranteed!"

—Sam Walton

The mark of a true professional is giving more than you get.
—Robert Kirby

The only certain avenue to success is to render more and better service than expected.
—Og Mandino

Our customers will begin to realize that they really can count on faster, crisper, more caring and personal service from us. That special relationship translates into real value for our customers—and when our customer wins, we win.
—Ron Kendrick

We love quality.
—Robert Campeau

Sign above each workbench in a toaster factory: "Careful, this may be the one your family gets."
—Great Ideas

Quality in our products and services is not a one-time "fix" that we install and forget. Quality is a perpetual mind-set—a complete, never-ending commitment by each person to improve our world and to live up to our agreements to one another.
—Dan Zadra

EXPECT

Promise a lot and give even more.
—Anythony J. D'Angelo

Quality and value first, followed by profit as a derivative. That is the hallmark of the most successful firms in any industry.
—Don Ward

Creating value for our customers doesn't just happen—it comes from spunk, energy, constant chatter, collaboration with our customers and imagination.
—Tom Peters

ACT WITH

INTEGRITY

Be true to your work and your word.

—Ben Morrow

Trust is a treasured item.
—Mary Augustine

To be trusted is a greater compliment than to be loved.
—George MacDonald

If you want to attract the best and the brightest, then you have to build an organization you feel good about.
—William C. Ford, Jr.

EXPECT

Tremendous humility comes from others having faith in you.

—Dag Hammerskjold

There can be no success or happiness if the things we believe in are different from the things we do.

—Freya Madeline Stark

It's important that people should know what you stand for. It is equally important that they know what you won't stand for.

—Mary Waldrin

People are beginning to see that the first requisite to success in business or in life is to be a good person.
—Herbert Spencer

A good head and a good heart are always a formidable combination.
—Nelson Mandela

Class is hard to define, but easy to recognize. It's being a good person, always taking responsibility and showing consideration for the consequences your actions have for others.
—Howard Ferguson

EXPECT

What is the quality of your intent?

—Thurgood Marshall

When I give the customer information, it is the truth. He may not want it, but it's the truth. And integrity means I'll be right there to stand behind it and help my customer through it.

—Chris Brillante

To children, integrity is keeping your promise. (Remember those famous words, "You promised!") To adults, it's doing what you say you do. (Remember those famous words, "Walking your talk.")

—Tom Pickett

It isn't common ground that bonds people together, it's higher ground.

—Tom Brown

Superior work teams recognize that consistently high performance can be built not on rules but only on values.

—Dennis Kinlaw

Thriving businesses succeed because their founders give something to their customers more precious than money, something that is a part of themselves. We sense this, appreciate it and, by becoming a customer, acknowledge and honor it.

—Paul Hawken

Hidden agendas destroy trust.
—Judith M. Bardwick

I have found that being open and honest is the best technique I can use. Right up front, tell people what you're trying to accomplish and what you're willing to sacrifice to accomplish it.
—Lee Iacocca

When we open up to the world around us, we open up the lines of communication. This communication enables us to hear and see things we never thought possible. Openness breeds communication, and communication holds the key to success.
—David Silverstein

The first rule: The Golden Rule.

—Jon Parks

More than a hundred years ago J.C. Penney launched his empire by hanging the Golden Rule above his door. If you think that's too old-fashioned for today's hardnosed executives, consider that a recent survey of Fortune 1500 execs found the most frequently mentioned success principle to be some variation of "Do unto others..."

—Don Ward

Treat all people with dignity and respect.

—John Wooden

We are remembered for what we do when it counts.

—Don Ward

American customers are reasonable and forgiving—unless we violate their trust. They don't expect us to deliver the moon, just deliver what we promised. They know our products won't always be perfect, but they expect us to stand behind them when they're not. Whatever we say on the outside—our advertising—needs to match with what we actually are on the inside. Integrity pays.

—Dan Zadra

HE BEST

"No limits; question everything; aim for the very best." That spirit is at the heart of the excellent organizations.

—Tom Peters

Believe me, there is no such thing as expecting too much.
—Susan Cheever

It's expectation that differentiates us from the dead.
—Sheila Ballantyne

We must not allow other people's limited perceptions to define us.
—Virginia Satir

There will always be a conflict between "good" and "good enough."
—Henry Martyn Leland

Half of success is thinking that what we are doing has got to be done the best anybody ever did it.
—Helen Gurley Brown

Great things are only possible with outrageous requests.
—Thea Alexander

Never leave well enough alone.
—Raymond Loewy

The achievement of excellence can only occur if the organization promotes a culture of creative dissatisfaction.
—Lawrence Miller

Progress is not created by contented people.
—Frank Tyger

You can't get there from "not here."
—Richard Moon

Great work is done by people who are not afraid to be great.
—Fernando Flores

We can scare ourselves or inspire ourselves. We are the architects of our own attitudes and experiences. We design the world by the way we choose to see it.
—Barry Neil Kaufman

Winning is a habit. Unfortunately, so is losing.

—Vince Lombardi

Once you say you're going to settle for second, that's what happens to you in life, I find.

—John F. Kennedy

If you want to be the best, you have to beat the best. If you aren't the best, you better find out in a hurry how good the best is, because that's how good you have to become. You can't be afraid of competition.

—Howard Ferguson

EXPECT

My competitors do more for me than my friends. My friends are often too polite to point out my weaknesses, but my competitors go to great expense to tell me all about them. My competitors are efficient and diligent. They drive me to constantly search for new ways to improve my products and services. My competitors would take my customers and market share away if they could. This keeps me alert, vigilant and proactive to steadily provide the best service possible. Each day I thank my competitors. They have been good to me. They sharpen my perceptions and help me grow.

—Lessons Learned, Service

SUCCESS

Aim so high you'll never be bored.
—Linda Gibbons

The urge for good design is inspiring—it's the same as the urge to go on living. The assumption is that somewhere, hidden, is a better way of doing things.
—Harry Bertoia

There are no such things as limits to growth, because there are no limits on the human capacity for intelligence, imagination and wonder.
—Ronald Reagan

We have to do the best we can. This is our sacred human responsibility.

—Albert Einstein

Care more than others think wise. Risk more than others think safe. Dream more than others think practical. Expect more than others think possible.

—Unknown

There is no penalty for overachievement.

—George W. Miller

STAGE

**Getting ready
is the secret
to success.**

—Henry Ford

Champions do not believe in chance.

—Rob Gilbert

You don't win games on optimism. You win games with preparation.

—Monte Clark

Luck is the residue of design.

—Branch Rickey

I can give you a six-word formula for success: "Think things through— then follow through."

—Edward Rickenbacker

If we are prepared, we have the edge. If we have the edge, we succeed.

—Jeanelle Anderson

Focused action beats brilliance any day.

—Art Turock

Begin with the end in mind.
—Richard Carlson, Ph.D.

Every moment spent planning saves three or four in execution.
—Crawford Greenwalt

Success is a science; if you have the conditions, you get the result.
—Oscar Wilde

Intellectuals solve problems; geniuses prevent them.
—Albert Einstein

Anticipate problems. An ounce of prevention is worth a pound of cure— and that's a return of sixteen to one!
—Larry Malinowski, Ph.D.

Design and prevention always beats inspection and rejection.
—Dan Zadra

Are you worried about pressure? I look at it this way: Pressure is nothing more than having to do something you are not totally prepared to do.

—Harvey Mackay

Nothing is as frightening as ignorance in action.

—Johann Wolfgang von Goethe

Winners worry about every little thing that can go wrong, but they feel less pressure because they do it sooner than their competition.

—Michael DeMarco

EXPECT

There is time for everything.
—Thomas Edison

*We have, and always have had,
all the time we need.*
—Melody Beattie

*Activity doesn't necessarily yield
achievement. Why work hard, only to
fail, when less work—systematically
directed—not only yields success,
but more free time as well?*
—Keynote

Business in general is an instinctive exercise in foresight.

—Henry Luce

Dreaming and seeing precede doing.

—Margaret E. Sangster

The way I see it, there are two kinds of dreams. One is a dream that's always going to be just that...a dream. Then there's a dream that's more than a dream, it's like...a map.

—Robert Cooper

EXPECT

Start with the vision; proceed with the plan.

—Dr. Larry Case

First comes thought; then organization of that thought into ideas and plans; then transformation of those plans into reality. Note that the beginning is always in your imagination.

—Napoleon Hill

Reappraise the past, reevaluate where we've been, clarify where we are, and predict or anticipate where we are headed. Then go.

—Toni Cade Bambara

SWEAT TH

E DETAILS

**Luck is infatuated
with the efficient.**

—Proverb

The difference between failure and success is doing a thing nearly right and exactly right.

—Edward C. Simmons

In all my years in sales and service I have never heard a customer say, "Jim, the thing I treasure about our relationship is that I can 'almost always' count on you to be there for me."

—Jim Williamson

It's not what we do now and then that counts—it's what we do every day, every time, and with every single customer that really counts.

—Ron Kendrick

Doing something is an accomplishment; doing something right is an achievement.

—Unknown

The difference between right and almost right is the difference between lightning and the lightning bug.

—Mark Twain

When you believe in something, and you carry it in your heart, you accept no excuses, only results.

—Ken Blanchard

Activity? Good. Productivity? Better.
—Old Maxim

*Why is there such a huge distance
between said and done?*
—Unknown

*Nothing is easier than being busy,
and nothing more difficult than
being effective.*
—Alec Mackenzie

EXPECT

There are no gold medals for the 95-yard dash.
—Max DePree

We are judged by what we finish, not by what we start.
—Susan Fielder

Don't tell me how hard you work. Tell me how much you get done.
—James Ling

There's a very thin line between successful people and unsuccessful ones; crossing over to the successful side requires only a subtle evolution in mindset.

—Gary Gabel

Successful people have formed the habit of doing the things that unsuccessful people don't like to do.

—Albert Gray

Commitment is critical for making changes. Let's make our deadlines and due dates mean something.

—Rhonda Abrams

Great things are a series of small things brought together.

—Vincent van Gogh

We don't try to be 100 percent better, rather 1 percent better a hundred ways.

—Ann Mitchell

Everyone in a company or team should believe that he or she has something to give to the organization which cannot otherwise be given.

—Dan Zadra

*From small beginnings come
great things.*
—Proverb

*You look at any giant corporation, and
I mean the biggies, and they all started
with a guy with an idea, doing it well.*
—Irv Robbins, Co-founder of Baskin Robbins

*Big companies are small companies
that succeed.*
—Robert Townsend

Pay attention to those details.
Sweat the small stuff.

—United Technologies

Character is what emerges from all
the little things you were too busy
to do yesterday, but did anyway.

—Mignon McLaughlin

Get a good idea and stay with it.
Dog it, and work at it until it's done,
and done right.

—Walt Disney

ROBLEM

*If your failure rate
is one in a million,
what do you tell
that one customer?*

—IBM

Expect problems and eat them for breakfast.
—Alfred A. Montapert

We have a problem. "Congratulations." But it's a tough problem. "Then double congratulations."
—W. Clement Stone

You only make mistakes if you're doing real work and getting things done.
—Carrol Tyler

Those who aren't making mistakes probably aren't making anything.
—Samuel Smiles

We are all failures at times—at least the best of us are.
—James M. Barrie

A mistake or problem with a project is an exception, and the mark of an exceptional company is how it treats its exceptions.
—Joe DeGeorge

Exploit a failure; don't waste it.

—Charles Kettering

A complaint is not a complaint—it's a golden opportunity to show your customer how much you really care.

—Bruce Nordstrom

Seek out and interrogate any unhappy customer. There is more good data in a mediocre complaint than in the best compliment.

—Jim Williamson

EXPECT

Make finding a solution and improving your service a higher priority than placing blame.

—Cathy Harrington

Even when we are not at fault, we must find a way to resolve the customer's problem. Taking responsibility and partnering with the customer to resolve their problem, regardless of its origin, builds customers for life.

—Paul Wirks

The goal is not to be right, it's to solve the problem and please our customer.

—C.D. Jackson

If things go wrong, don't go with them.
—Roger Babson

*The first rule for success? Show up.
Don't avoid.*
—Jeanne Robertson

*It is important to acknowledge a
mistake instantly, correct it, and learn
from it. That literally turns a failure
into a success. Success is on the far
side of failure.*
—T.J. Watson

EXPECT

What is it going to be—reasons or results?
—Art Turock

When you bring a problem, bring a solution.
—John Gilles

The secret is to gang up on the problem, rather than each other.
—Thomas Stallkamp, Chrysler

Goodwill is the one and only asset that competition cannot undersell or destroy.

—Marshall Field

An argument is always about what has been made more important than the relationship.

—Hugh Prather

Remember that problems are a normal part of doing business. Problems come and go, but goodwill and the relationship should last and last.

—Cat Lane

A survey of Fortune 500 buyers isolates 25 factors influencing the quality of the customer relationship. Honest communication is second only to quality. It's just this simple: If there's a problem, say so. If you need a 30-minute meeting, don't ask for 15. Always tell it like it is. Say what you mean. Say exactly what you mean. Say only what you mean.

—Great Ideas

SUCCESS

ATE OPENLY

The magic is to get people communicating on a personal level. Who knows, we might even end up liking each other.

—Danett Lee

The word communication comes from the Latin "communico" meaning, "to come together, to share."
—Michael Nolan

Many people think they are communicating with their customers or teammates, when in fact all they are doing is telling or informing.
—Frank Vizzare

"Information" and "communication" are often used interchangeably, but they signify quite different things. Information is giving out; communication is getting through.
—Sydney J. Harris

True communication is an open bridge that works both ways. When we build bridges we can keep crossing them.

—Jane Alvarez

We want to spark real conversations with our customers, alert them to ways we can help them, not browbeat them to buy.

—Anita Roddick, The Body Shop

Make your customer feel heard and understood. Make your customer feel appreciated and helped. Understand that you can do none of these things unless you listen carefully to your customers and sincerely care about them.

—Kay R. Smith

Being in front of our customer doesn't help if we do all the talking.

—Beth Klein

Before I can provide
What John Jones buys,
I must see the world
Through John Jones' eyes.

—Old Maxim

Openness means being willing to check your personal ego at the door, so you can listen to someone else's input. It's listening at higher levels—not just with the ears, but often with the heart.

—Michelle Druckhammer

Empathy is patiently and sincerely seeing the world through the other person's eyes. It is not learned in school; it is cultivated over a lifetime.
—Albert Einstein

What we most care for, what we most need to do, is right there— when we take the time to listen.
—Jack Kornfield

When Disneyland opened, Walt Disney's assistants were concerned because the guests were walking on the new grass. Disney replied, "They're telling you where they want you to put the paths."
—Diane Kerdock

Consumers are statistics.
Customers are people.

—Stanley Marcus

As companies grow they tend to treat
people like numbers, and confuse
services with service.

—Dan Zadra

To the bank you're a "depositor."
To the power company you're a
"rate payer." To the insurance
company you're a "policyholder."
To the direct mail company you're
an "entry." To the politician you're
a "constituent." And the sad thing
is, they often treat you that way,
don't they?

—Lessons Learned, Service

When customers leave us for greener pastures, they usually give price as the reason, when in fact it's simple neglect.

Customers feel we take them for granted; only show interest when we want an order; lavish our time on prospects; communicate mainly by invoice; are fixated on "big accounts;" drop them like hot potatoes once we have the order; don't follow through on promises; and satisfy our own bureaucracy rather than their needs. We can do better than that, much better.

—John R. Graham

"How can I help you?" is a question we ask our customers every day; I believe it's a question we should be asking our co-workers and teammates every day, as well.

—Ron Kendrick

Every routine eye-to-eye contact with the customer is a "Moment of Truth." It's a golden opportunity for each of us to personally demonstrate the unique spirit and service of our company.

—Scott Johnson

If we make our customers important, they will inevitably return the favor.

—Don Ward

Every time I answer the phone, the customer on the other end becomes the most important person on earth.

—Elizabeth Dalton

Instead of "I don't know," say "I'll find out." Instead of "You'll have to," say, "Here's how I can help you." Instead of "Hang on for a second," say, "Are you able to hold for a minute while I check?" Instead of, "We can't do that," say, "That's a tough one, but let's see what we can do."

—Jim Williamson

IMAGINE THE

POSSIBILITIES

To be a success in business, be daring, be first, be different.

—Marchant

The future belongs to those who see possibilities before they become obvious.

—John Sculley

Be the antidote for all the unoriginal thinking that's going on around you.

—Delores Rodriguez

New ideas are the lifeblood of every company. Remember the story of the starving man who did a brilliant job of weeding his garden. Unfortunately he never planted a thing in his life.

—Tom Peters

Without leaps of imagination or dreaming, we lose the excitement of possibilities. Dreaming, after all, is a form of planning.

—Gloria Steinem

Where we cannot invent, we may at least improve.

—Colton

Originality is not necessarily doing something no one else has ever done, but doing what has been done countless times with new life, new breath.

—Marie Chapian

Everything is always impossible before it works.

—Hunt Greene

What we have before us are some breathtaking opportunities disguised as insoluble problems.

—John W. Gardner

Every new idea goes through three stages: It won't work...It will cost too much...I thought it was a good idea all along.

—Rick Finn

I am looking for a lot of people who have an infinite capacity to not know what can't be done.
—Henry Ford

Some of the world's greatest feats were accomplished by people not smart enough to know they were impossible.
—Doug Larson

One of the saddest lines is, "Be realistic." The best parts of this world were fashioned by people who dared to look hard at their wishes and gave them horses to ride.
—Richard N. Bolles

Normal is not something to aspire to, it's something to get away from.

—Jodie Foster

Do not quench your inspiration and your imagination; do not become the slave of your model.

—Vincent van Gogh

The conventional view only serves to protect us from the painful job of thinking.

—J.K. Galbraith

The people in every competitive company are in a career development class every day.

—Tom Brown

We have learned to relish imagination and change. I will go anywhere to talk to people who say they are doing things in a better way.

—Anita Roddick, The Body Shop

It had long since come to my attention that people of accomplishment rarely sat back and let things happen to them. They went out and happened to things.

—Elinor Smith

Possibilities do not add up.
They multiply.
—Paul M. Romer

That's the beautiful thing about
innovation. Just get it started in your
company, and suddenly one idea is
leading to another.
—Roger von Oech

Ideas are like rabbits. You get a
couple, learn how to handle them,
and pretty soon you have a dozen.
—John Steinbeck

EXPECT

Just keep questioning the status quo. See things as you would have them be, instead of as they are.

—Robert Collier

As a nation, we Americans disrespect the status quo and have a historical bent for reinvention. It is, arguably, our greatest strength and distinction. We'll try anything and we're not afraid to fail—which sets us apart from our economic competitors. American business hasn't got it perfect. But as long as we revel in our disorderliness and raucously debate the way forward, there's hope.

—Tom Peters

TRUST YO

UR TEAM

Hire people smarter than you are and get out of their way.

—Howard Schultz, Starbucks

Good leaders surround themselves with good people.

—Unknown

People are not our most important asset. The right people are.

—Jim Collins

Creativity. Passion. Commitment. Those are the qualities that companies need most if they want to win in the new world of business. Those are also the qualities that are lacking at most companies.

—Jim Stuart

We need more HOW thinkers,
not IF thinkers.

—Frank Vizzare

The best leaders are not interested in
selling their own ideas, but in finding
the best ideas. They are not interested
in having their own way, but in finding
the best way.

—Commitment to Teamwork

Set your expectations high; find men
and women whose integrity and values
you respect; get their agreement on a
course of action; and give them your
ultimate trust.

—John Akers

Excellent organizations do not foster "we and they" attitudes.

—Tom Peters

My idea of a successful meeting is when somebody attends and says, "I couldn't tell who worked for whom."

—Chuck Beyer

A strong leader does not ask people to serve him, but the common end. A strong leader has not followers, but men and women working with him.

—Mary Parker Follett

EXPECT

Teamwork means never having to say, "That's not my job." It means I'll be there at any time you need my help, and I'll do my best to help you do your job in any way I can.

—John Ablakat

A boss says, "Go!" A leader says, "Let's go!"

—E. M. Kelley

The best leaders try to train their followers themselves to become leaders. They wish to be leaders of leaders.

—Mary Parker Follett

To build a great team: 1) Do what you say. 2) Treat people the way you want to be treated. 3) Treat all people the same.

—Jim Wilson

What Diversity "problem?" Diversity creates one and only one thing: opportunity.

—Tom Peters

Great companies respect their customers and employees—people at all levels and from all backgrounds. By showing respect for others, an organization itself becomes respected. It rises in stature, and makes a positive impact on the world.

—James Collins

EXPECT

I believe every person has the ability to achieve something important, and with that in mind I regard everyone as special, and I treat them that way.

—Mary Kay Ash

Everyone who does the best he or she can do is a hero.

—Josh Billings

When people act heroically, treat them like heroes. Throw the spotlight into every nook and cranny of your organization and catch people in the act of doing something right.

—Bill Meyer

Bureaucracy is the opposite of teamwork, the opposite of a healthy organization. Bureaucracy is nothing more than the hardening of an organization's arteries.
—William P. Anthony

Bureaucrats are against everything and for nothing.
—Emilio Agosti

If you have a Don't Manual in your company, toss it in the waste basket and replace it with a Do Manual. No company ever got anywhere by being anti-everything. Be for something!
—Don Ward

Reward excellent failures.
Punish mediocre successes.

—Phil Daniels

The only advantage over competitors
is the brain power you have in your
own organization.

—Ralph Stayer

If you took all of Microsoft's buildings,
real estate, office hardware, physical
assets—anything you can touch—away
from the company, where would it be?
Almost exactly where it is now because
in today's world a company's value is in
its thinking, not its possessions.

—Steve Chandler

ENJOY TH

JOURNEY

Life is too short to be cranky.

—Beej Whiteaker-Hawks

*The supreme achievement is to blur
the line between work and play.*
—Arthur Toynbee

*If you love what you do, you will never
work another day in your life.*
—Confucius

*I urge all company leaders to come to
work first, before anyone else shows
up, and trot onto and off of the mound.
Your personal display of energy and
zest for your task, your product,
your customers, the people you work
with and life in general is the single
most important determinant of your
organization's "hum."*
—Tom Peters

It's so hard when I have to, and so easy when I want to.

—Sondra Anice Barnes

I see people who can't wait to get to work to see what's going to happen next. I see people in meetings, with tough tasks and goals, smiling and laughing and keeping a sense of humor with all the seriousness around them. Everyone enjoys doing what they like most, their purpose, their work.

—Tom Pickett

Customers love people who have fun doing their job. It's a contagious effect which makes the service experience unforgettably positive for us all.

—Beth Drake

Tickle your mind.

—Lindsey Collier

What is central to business is the joy of creating.

—Peter Robinson

In sports, the edge is in the brain, not the body. In business, the edge is in the heart, not the brain. In life, the edge is in relishing the achieving, not the achievement.

—Unknown

EXPECT

Having fun is not a diversion from a successful life; it is the pathway to it.
—Martha Beck

When we don't enjoy what we do, we only nick the surface of our potential.
—Dennis Wholey

Creativity is inventing, experimenting, growing, taking risks, breaking rules, making mistakes, and having fun.
—Mary Lou Cook

The real secret of joy in work is contained in one word—excellence. To know how to do something well is to enjoy it.

—Pearl Buck

Excellence is not merely a skill. It is an attitude.

—Ralph Marston

Help each other be right, not wrong. Look for ways to make new ideas work, not for reasons they won't work.

—Ian Percy

Instead of "That could be a problem,"
think "That could be an opportunity."
Instead of "Let somebody else
deal with it," think "I'm ready
to learn something new."
Instead of "I'm too busy,"
think "I'll make time."
Instead of "It can't be done,"
think "There's always a way."
Instead of "Let's see what happens,"
think "Let's make it happen."
Instead of "That's the way we've
always done it," think
"Let's find a better way."
Instead of "I don't have any idea,"
think "Let's explore some alternatives."
Instead of "It will never fly," think
"We'll never know until we try."

—Unknown

When someone does something good, applaud! You will make two people happy.
—Samuel Goldwyn

If you think a complimentary thought about someone, don't just think it, write it down and pass it on. Dare to compliment people and pass on compliments to them from others.
—Catherine Ponder

To every leader and manager: In the next 96 hours, send four thank-you notes to front-line employees for a job well done; repeat every 96 hours thereafter, for the rest of your life. Repeat the same process with your customers.
—Tom Peters

EXPECT

What a lot we lost when we stopped writing letters! You can't reread a phone call.

—Liz Carpenter

At my retirement party several people came up to me, one or two with tears in their eyes, and thanked me for a thank-you note, sometimes one I'd written 10 or 15 years before.

—3M Executive

In the end there is an applause superior to that of the multitude— one's own.

—Elizabeth Elton Smith

ROWING

Thou hast seen nothing yet.

—Miguel de Cervantes

There is no finish line.

—Nike Motto

You get out in front—you stay out in front.

—A.J. Foyt, Race Car Driver

No matter how big or successful you are, if you stop being the scrappy underdog, fighting against the odds, you risk sliding into the worst fate of all: mediocrity.

—Howard Schultz, Starbucks

EXPECT

The secret to a rich life is to have more beginnings than endings.

—Dave Weinbaum

It isn't where we came from; it's where we're going that counts.

—Ella Fitzgerald

There are far, far better things ahead than any we leave behind.

—C.S. Lewis

The only menace is inertia.
—St. John Perse

*The first rule of survival is clear:
Nothing is more dangerous than
yesterday's success.*
—Alvin Toffler

*Effective management begins with the
inability to leave well enough alone,
with a preoccupation for betterment.*
—Priscilla Elfrey

Which is stronger: our urge to grow or our resistance to change?
—Mark D. Erickson

Let's build a future—not just polish the past.
—Frank Vizzare

Each destination you reach only opens out into wider horizons, new and undiscovered countries for you to explore.
—Barbara Sher with Annie Gottlieb

We always underestimate the future.

—Charles Kettering

The growth of the human mind is still high adventure, in many ways the highest adventure on earth.

—Norman Cousins

My concern is not just about surviving. I will not live at any cost. My attempt is to do better than just survive, but to thrive. And to thrive with some passion, some compassion, some humor and some style.

—Maya Angelou

EXPECT

The future is not something we enter, it's something we create.

—Leonard I. Sweet

If an organization is to meet the challenges of a changing world, it must be prepared to change everything about itself except its core values.

—Thomas Watson, Jr.

For things to change, we must change. For things to get better, we must get better.

—Heidi Wills

*The moment you stop learning,
you stop leading.*

—Rick Warren

*Leadership is not something that we
learn once and for all. It is an ever-
evolving pattern of skills, talents, and
ideas that grow and change as we do.*

—Sheila Murray Bethel

*All great organizations are learning
organizations; they are students of
past mistakes who benefit from all
that has gone before.*

—Normand L. Frigon

EXPECT

Even last month's manual should be out of date.

—Taiichi Ohno, Toyota

For changes to occur, you have to embrace them over and over. Take it step by step—but keep moving forward—and a year from now, you'll find you've moved from here to there.

—Rhonda Abrams

That's what education means— to be able to do what you've never done before.

—George Herbert Palmer

Keep dreaming, wishing and planning.
There's immeasurable power in it.
—Laura Smith

Trends will come and trends will go,
but meeting the needs of our customer,
taking care of our employees, and
being responsible to the communities
in which we live and work are basic
values that will never go out of style.
—Brian D. Perkins

Your Mission is meaningful and
important not just to your company,
but to your community. You can't
let it become just a bunch of nice-
sounding words on a piece of paper.
It must become and remain a clear and
compelling call to action.
—Dan Zadra

EXPECT

If success is not on your own terms, if it looks good to the world but does not feel good in your heart, it is not success at all.

—Anna Quindlen

I don't think there's any right way or wrong way to run a business...but if there is a monument to be made, it's to the values that are instilled in the business. And hopefully those values will live long after any of us leaves.

—Harry V. Quadracci

When we're in our nineties and we're looking back, it's not going to be how much money we made or how many awards we've won. It's really, "What did we stand for? Did we make a positive difference for people?"

—Elizabeth Dole

Also available from Compendium Publishing are these spirited and compelling companion books of great quotations.

Be Happy.
Remember to Live, Love,
Laugh and Learn

Be the Difference

Because of You™
Celebrating the Difference
You Make™

Brilliance™
Uncommon Voices From
Uncommon Women™

**Commitment to
Excellence™**
Celebrating the Very Best

Everyone Leads™
It takes each of us to make a
difference for all of us™

Forever Remembered™
A Gift for the Grieving Heart™

I Believe in You™
To your heart, your dream and
the difference you make

Little Miracles™
To renew your dreams,
lift your spirits, and strengthen
your resolve™

Reach for the Stars™
Give up the Good to Go
for the Great

Thank You
In appreciation of you,
and all that you do.

To Your Success™
Thoughts to Give Wings to
Your Work and Your Dreams™

Together We Can™
Celebrating the power of
a team and a dream™

Whatever It Takes™
A Journey into the Heart
of Human Achievement™

You've Got a Friend™
Thoughts to Celebrate
the Joy of Friendship™

These books may be ordered directly from the publisher
(800) 914-3327. But please try your bookstore first!

www.compendiuminc.com